Sometimes It Scares Me

Words by
Judith Conaway

Pictures by
Katie Maloney

Raintree Editions

Design/Paul Westermann

Copyright © 1977, Raintree Publishers Limited

All rights reserved. No part of this book may be reproduced or utilized in any form or by any means, electronic or mechanical, including photocopying, recording, or by any information storage and retrieval system, without permission in writing from the Publisher. Inquiries should be addressed to Raintree Publishers Limited, 205 West Highland Avenue, Milwaukee, Wisconsin 53203.

Library of Congress Number: 76-46342

2 3 4 5 6 7 8 9 0 81 80 79 78

Printed in the United States of America.

Published by

Raintree Editions
A Division of Raintree Publishers Limited
Milwaukee, Wisconsin 53203

Distributed by

Childrens Press
1224 West Van Buren Street
Chicago, Illinois 60607

Library of Congress Cataloging in Publication Data

Conaway, Judith, 1948-
  Sometimes it scares me.

  SUMMARY: Explores the things that can frighten children and how these fears may be overcome.
  1. Fear in children — Juvenile literature.
[1. Fear] I. Maloney, Katie. II. Title.
BF723.F4C65   152.4   76-46342
ISBN 0-8172-0060-6 lib. bdg.

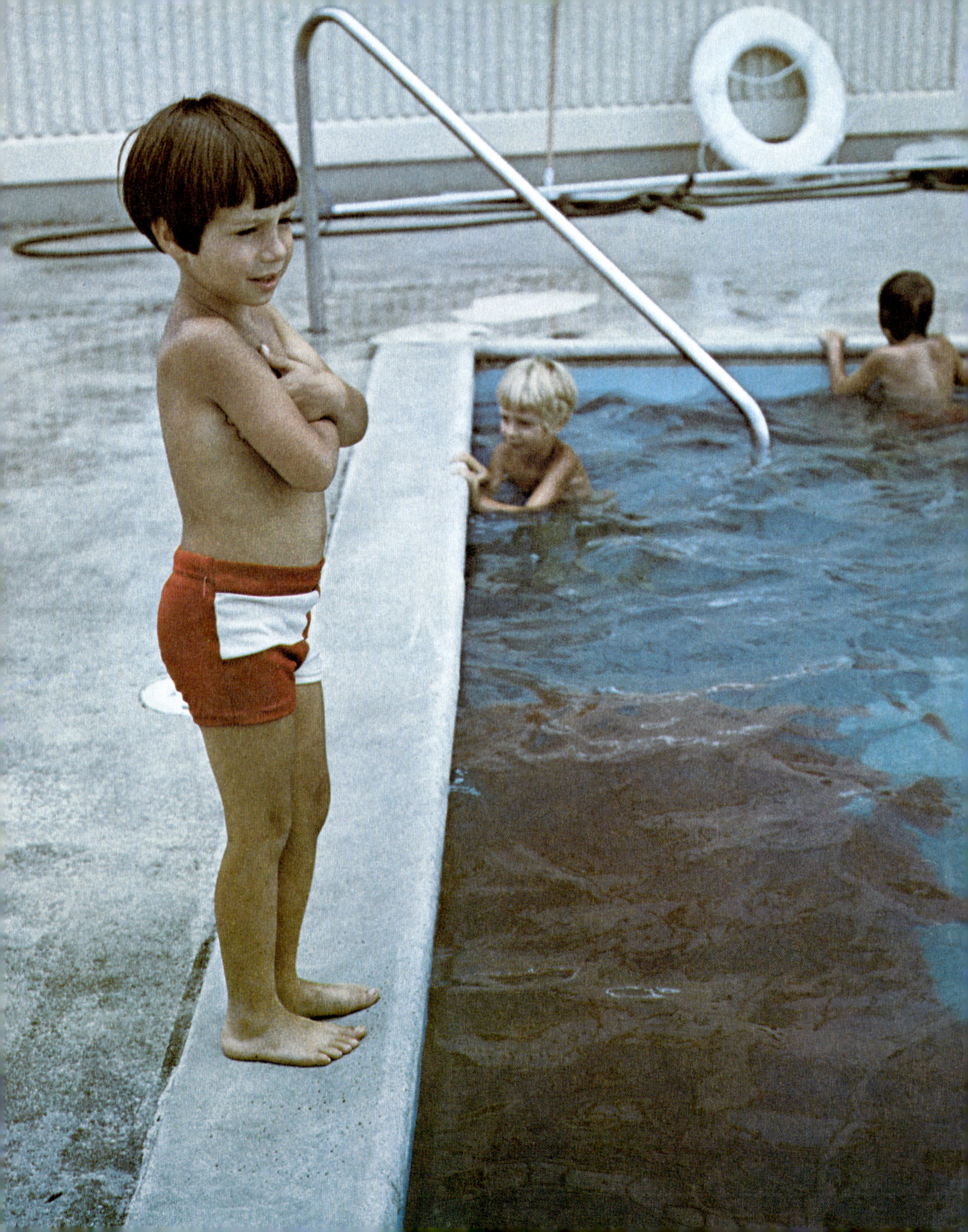

Hi. My name is Ben. I am six years old. That means I'm almost grown up. But sometimes things still scare me.

I took my first swimming lessons this summer. On the first day, I was afraid to go into the water. I just stood on the edge of the pool. The water looked awfully deep.

My brother Tim was already in the pool.

"Hey, Ben," he called. "What's the matter? You scared?"

I didn't say anything. I just sat down. I was afraid all right. The water was deep. It was cold too. I didn't want to go in at all. But I was afraid Tim would laugh at me if I stayed out. So I made myself get in the water.

It wasn't so bad once I got used to it. But I hung onto the side of the pool for a long time.

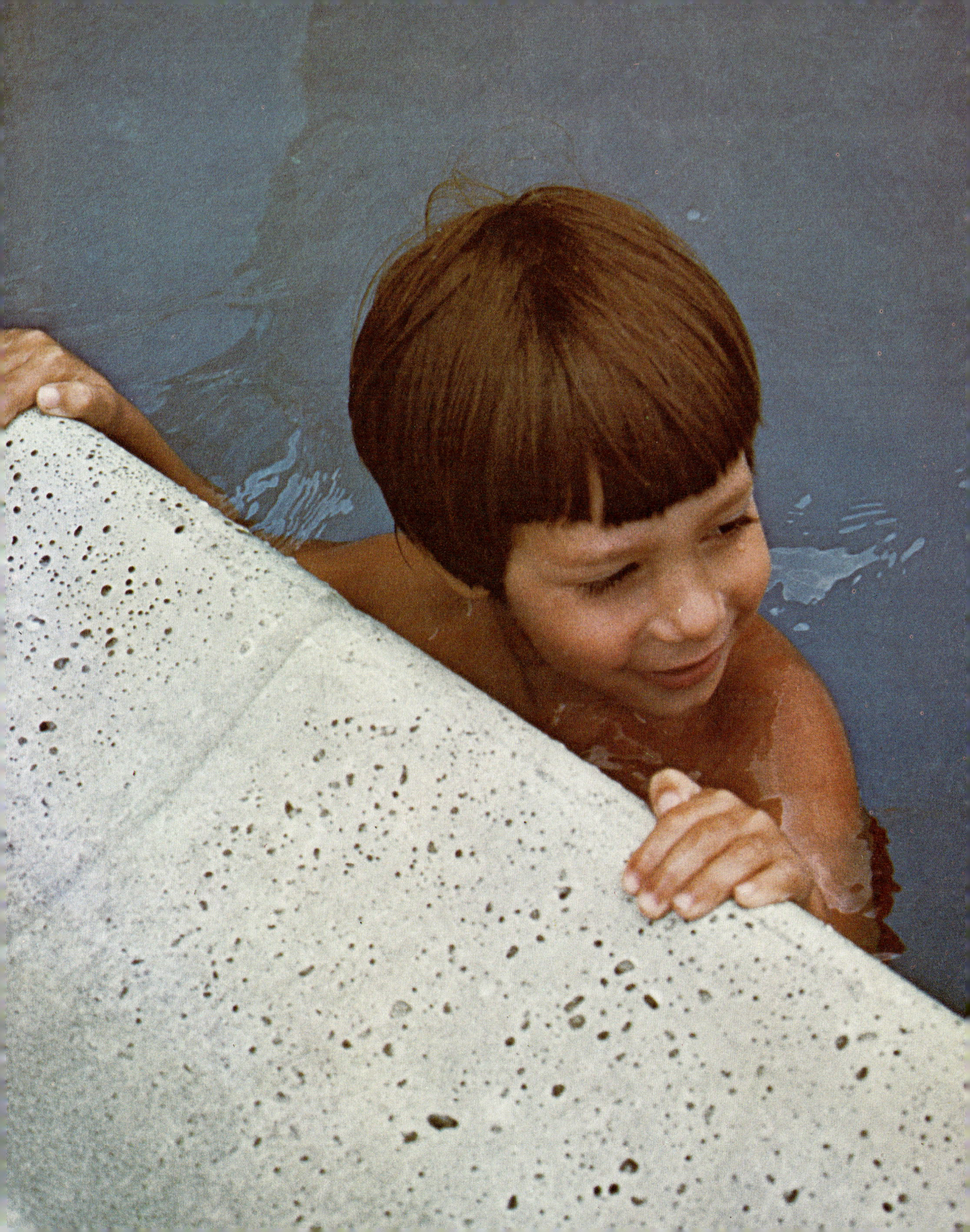

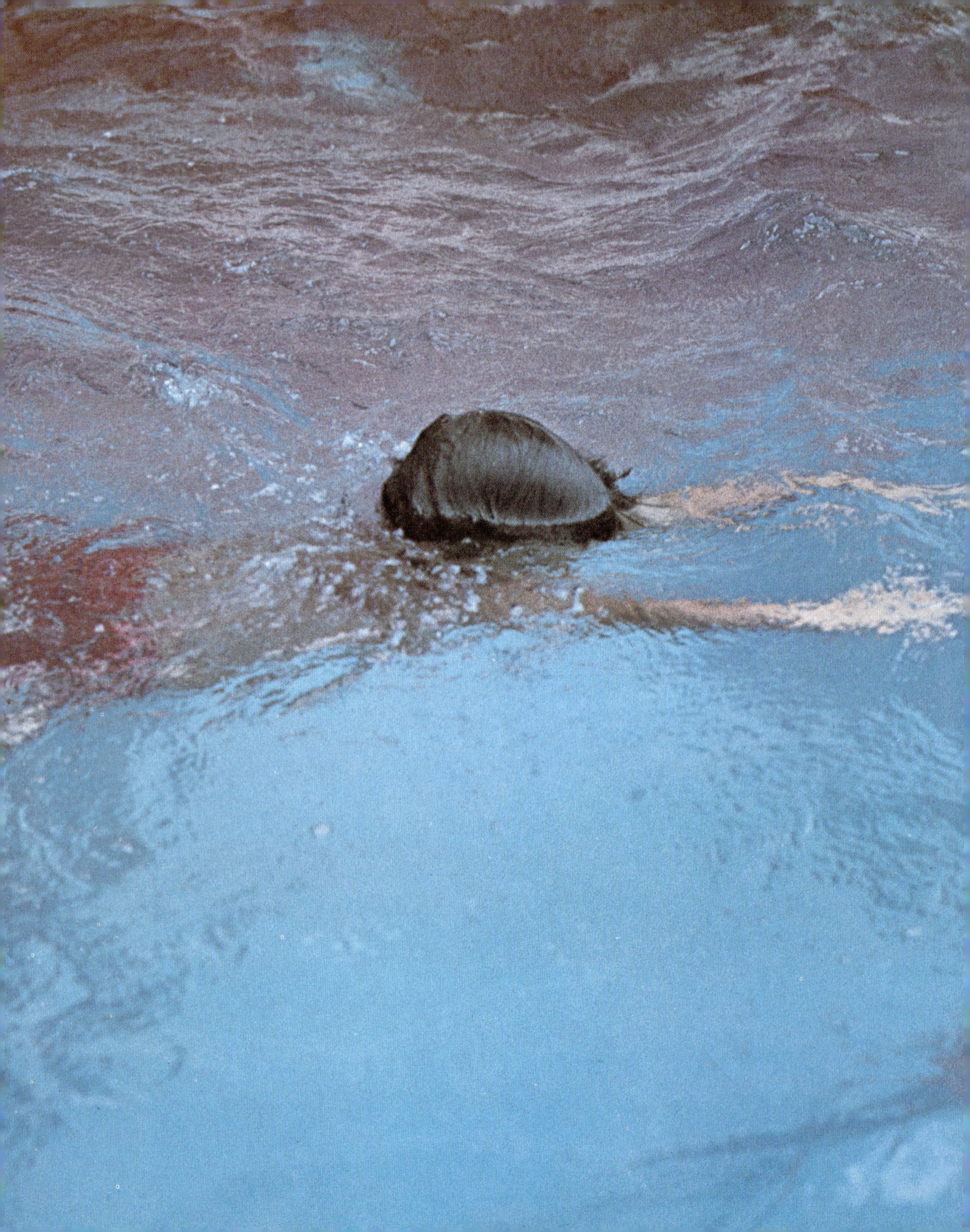

At the next lesson, I learned how to float. Floating was hard at first. I was afraid that I would sink. I was really frightened when I went under the water.

But my teacher showed me how to float right. She held onto me until I could float by myself.

It wasn't long before I could paddle by myself too.

I am not afraid of the water now. I think I was frightened because I had never been swimming before. Sometimes it scares me to do new things. I can't help it.

I'm not the only one who gets scared. Tim does too. One time we all went downtown to a big store. After a while, my mom asked, "Where's Tim?" I didn't know where he was.

We looked all around, but we couldn't see him. At last we found him. He had gotten lost in the store. Boy, was he glad to see us! He was really scared.

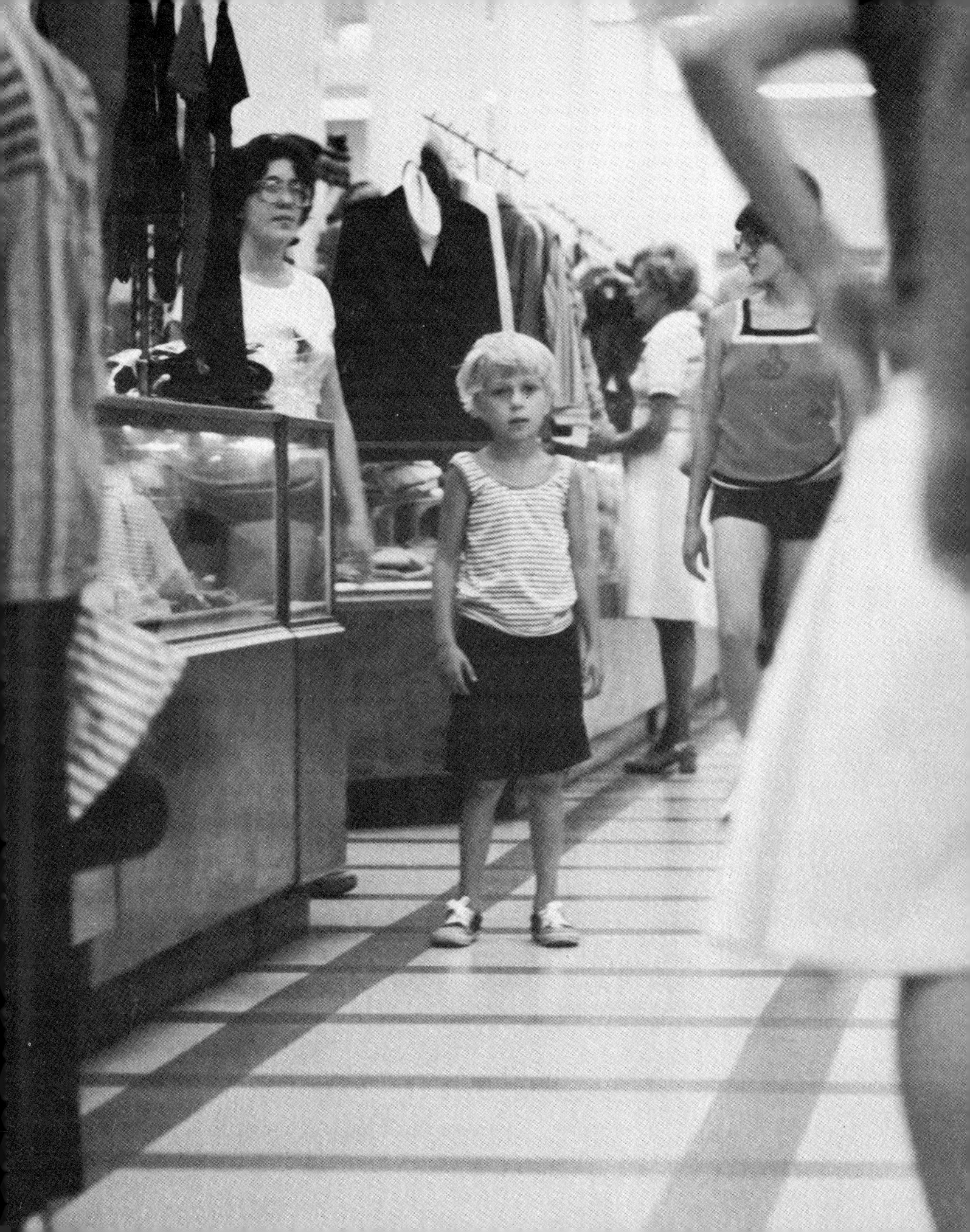

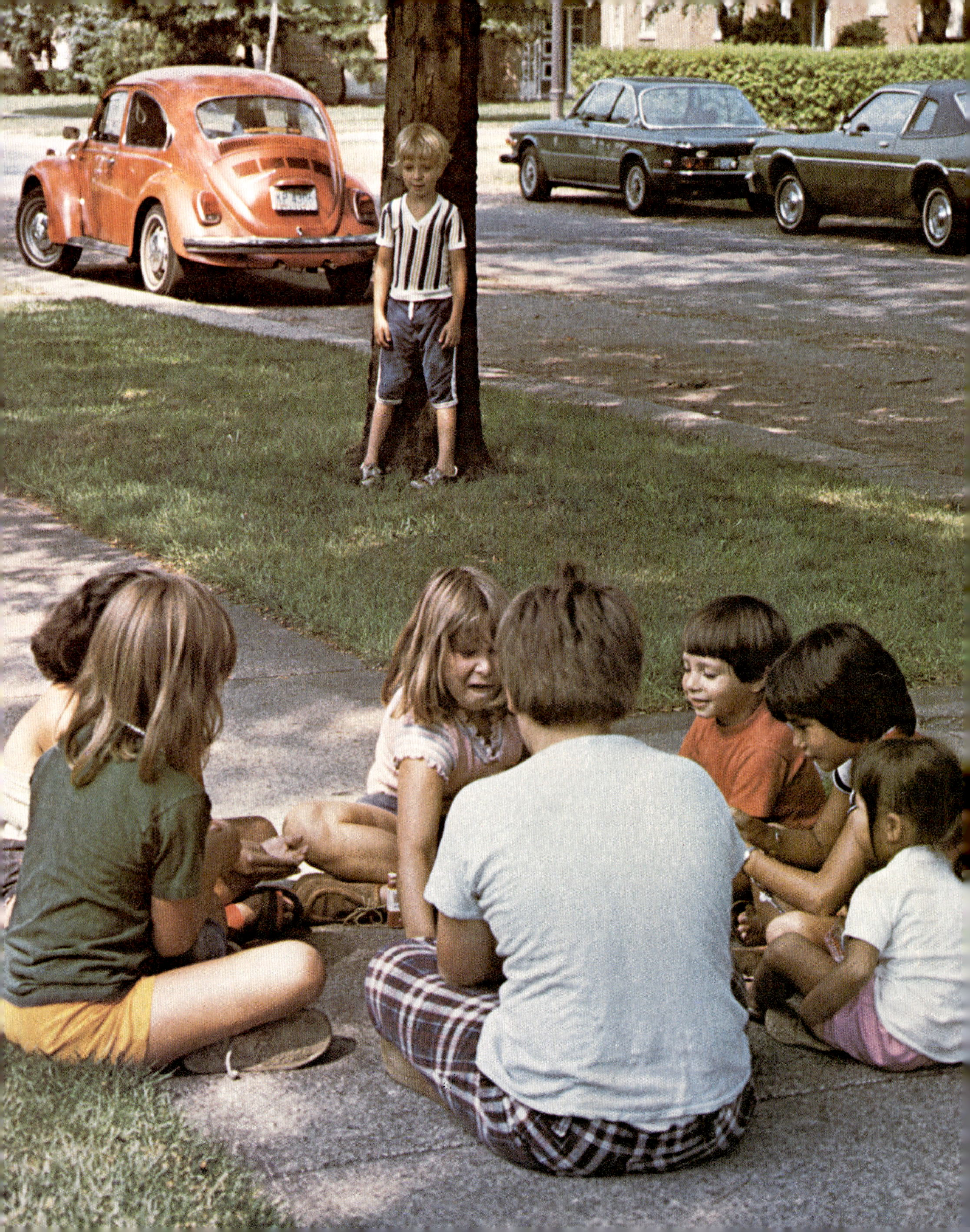

Different things scare different people. Tim is afraid to talk to people. My mom says that's because he's shy. One time we were all outside playing a game. Tim was outside too. He stood a long way off. He wouldn't come near us.

After a while, he came a little bit closer. He wanted to see what we were doing.

Then someone said, "Want to play, Tim?"

And Tim said, "Sure."

That's the way Tim is. You have to ask him to play with you. Boy, it must be hard to be shy. I'm not shy at all. But sometimes when I play with the other kids, I get scared too. I wonder what they really think of me. Do they like me? Do they hate me? Do they think I'm good enough for them? Do they laugh at me when I am not there? Sometimes I'm just a little afraid of other people.

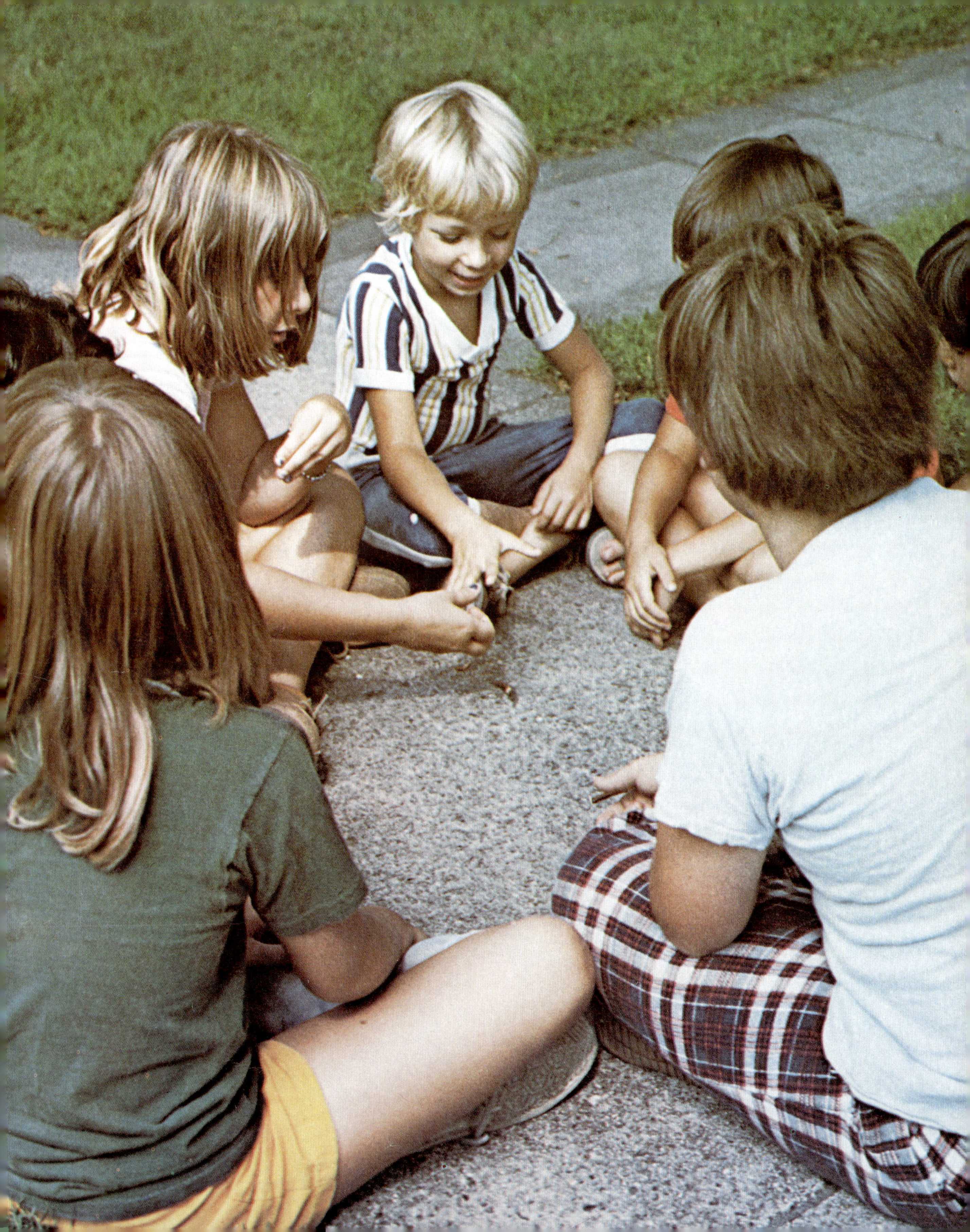

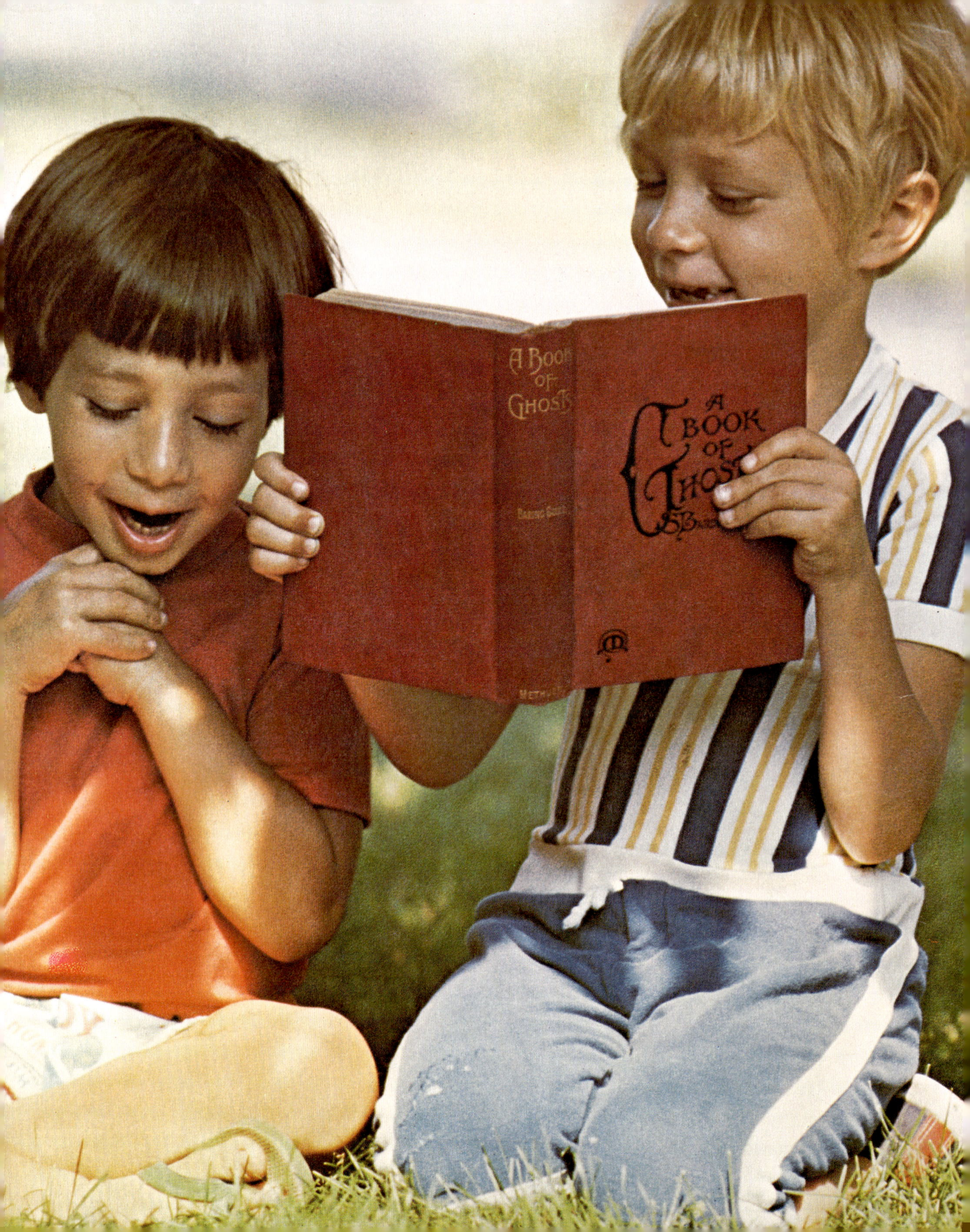
A BOOK OF GHOSTS
A BOOK OF

But what I'm really afraid of is ghosts.

Once Tim went to the library. He got this old book of ghost stories. Boy, were they creepy.

There was one story about some people who lived way out in the country. They had a ghost in their house. It was the ghost of a dead pirate. He kept his treasure in their house. The ghost wanted to scare the people away.

There was a picture of the pirate ghost in the book. Wow, it looked mean and ugly. The ghost was white. It had a black patch over one eye. It had one giant tooth.

That night I stayed up really late to read the book. Then I fell asleep.

Did you ever get really scared by a dream? Well, I was scared that night. In my dream the pirate ghost came to steal me away. I tried to get away. But I couldn't run fast enough.

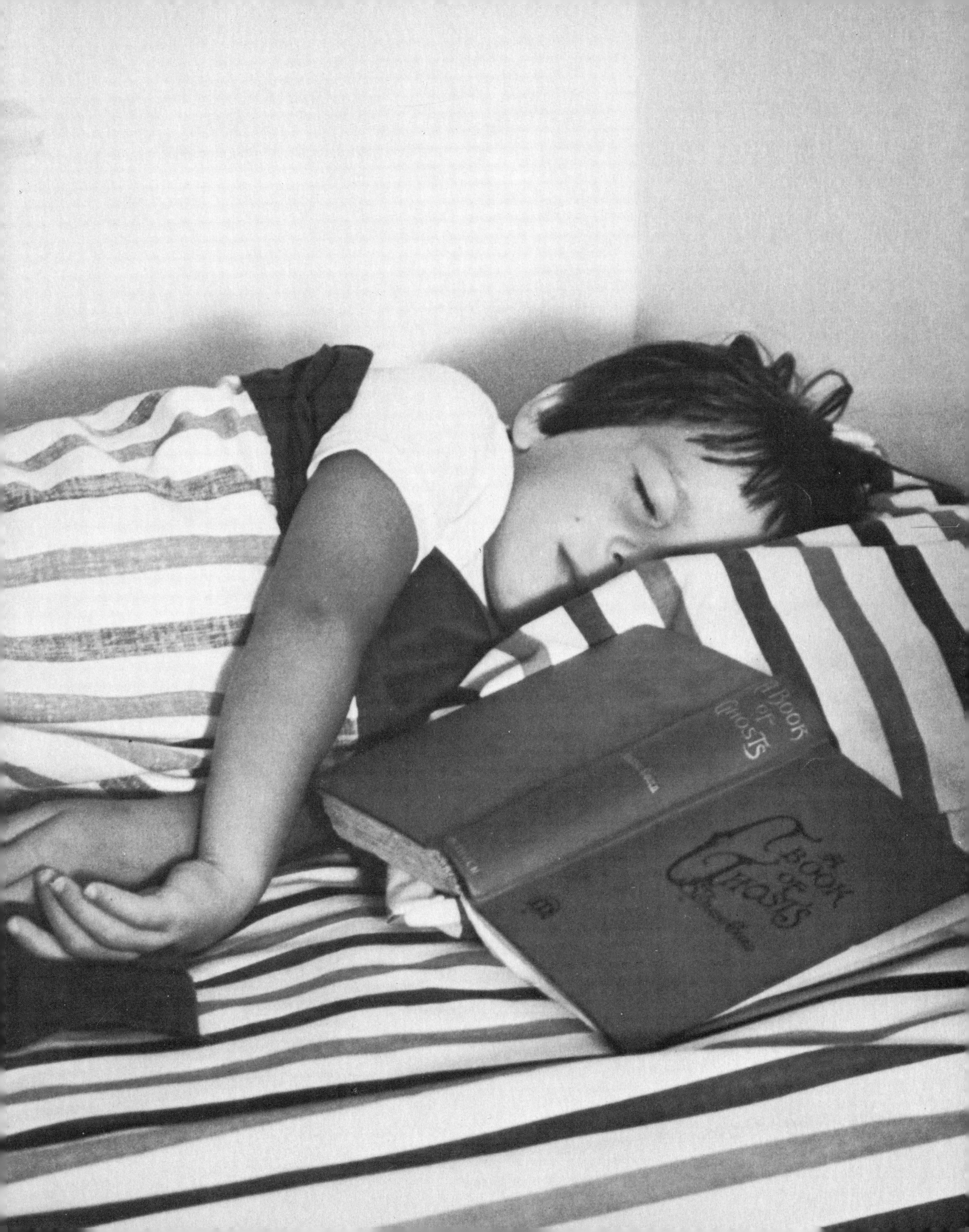
A BOOK OF GHOSTS

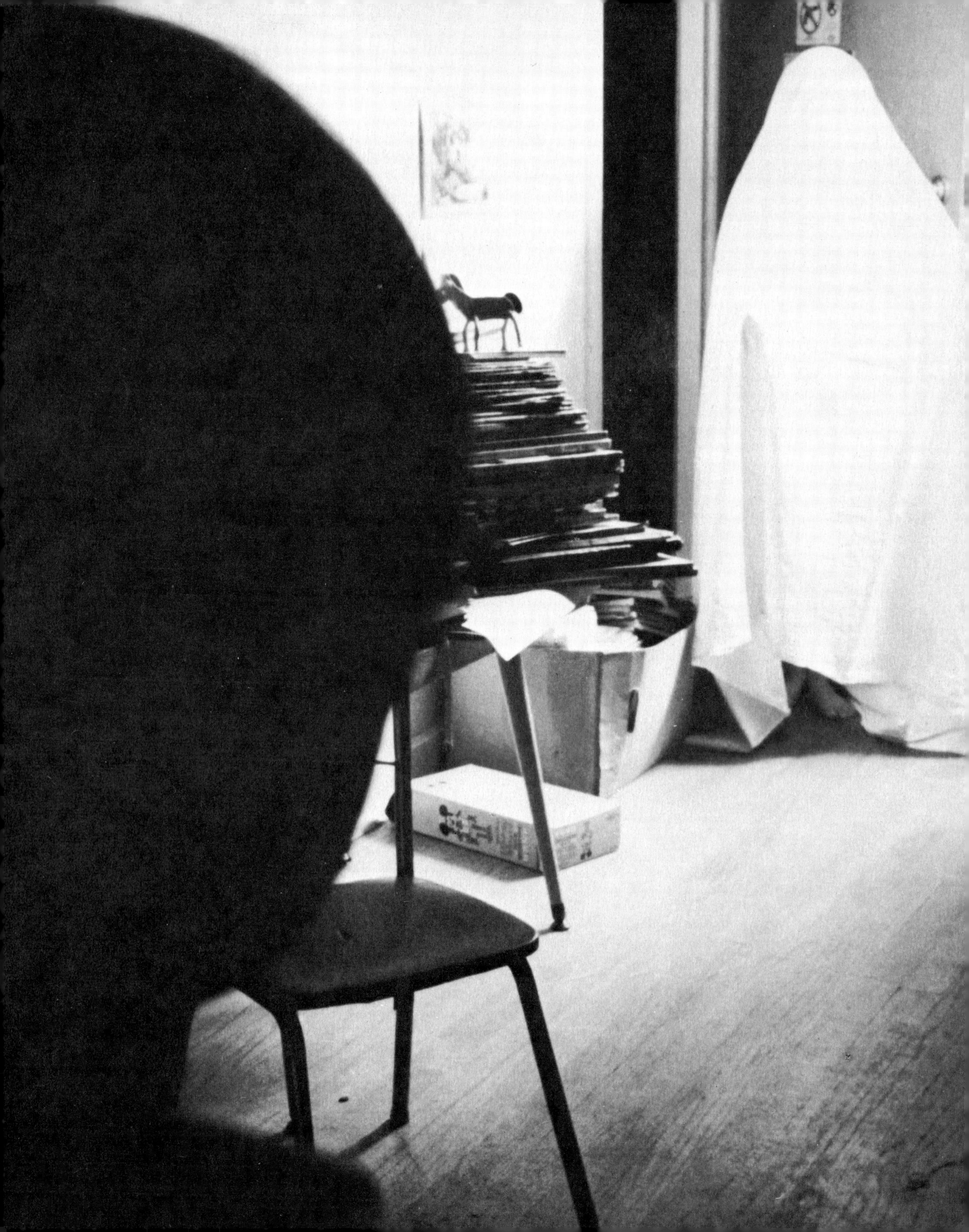

There was a loud noise in the room. I woke up. I sat up to see what the noise was. It was a ghost! I was so frightened. I screamed and screamed.

But then I saw that it was only Tim. He was laughing at me. I guess it was pretty funny — for him. He really did scare me that time.

I was angry with Tim. I wanted to get even. So I bought a toy spider. It was only plastic, but it looked real. I put it on the grass right next to Tim. Boy, did he let out a scream!

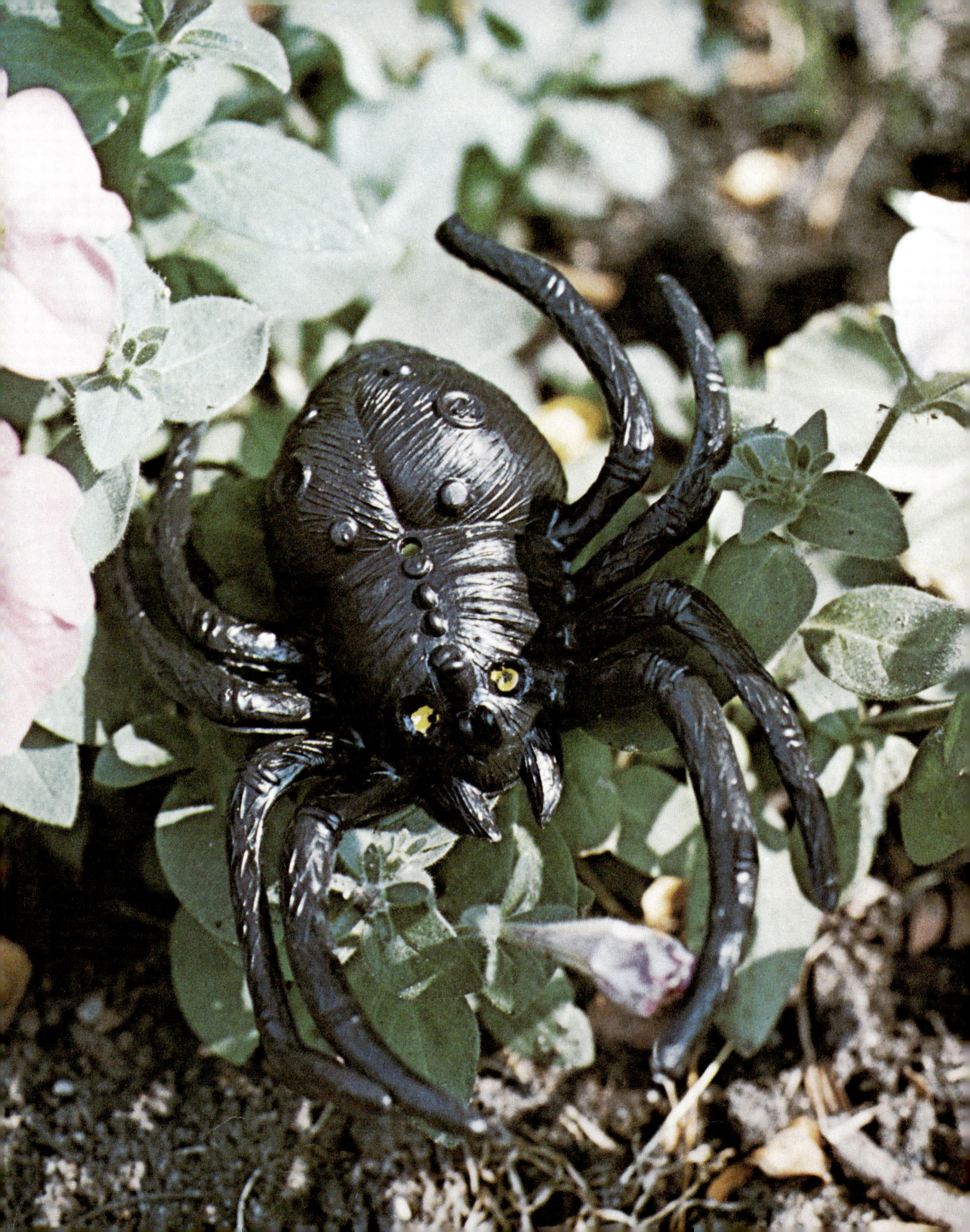

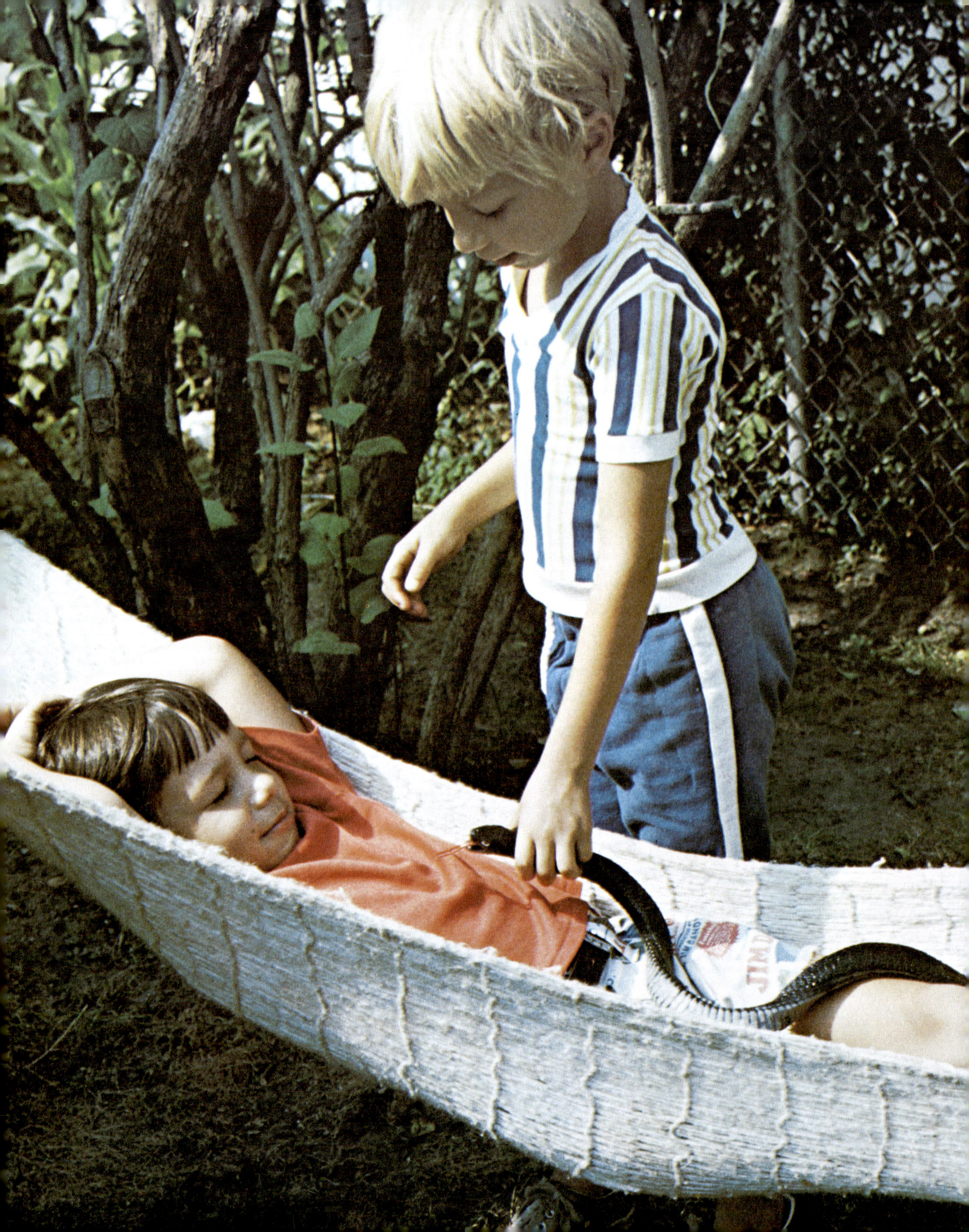

Well, I knew he would try to get back at me for that. The next day I was lying outside in the sun. I heard someone coming, so I pretended to be asleep.

It was Tim. He had a big rubber snake. He was going to scare me with it. I kept my eyes closed.

Then I pretended to wake up. I started laughing.
"Ha, ha! You didn't scare me!" I said.

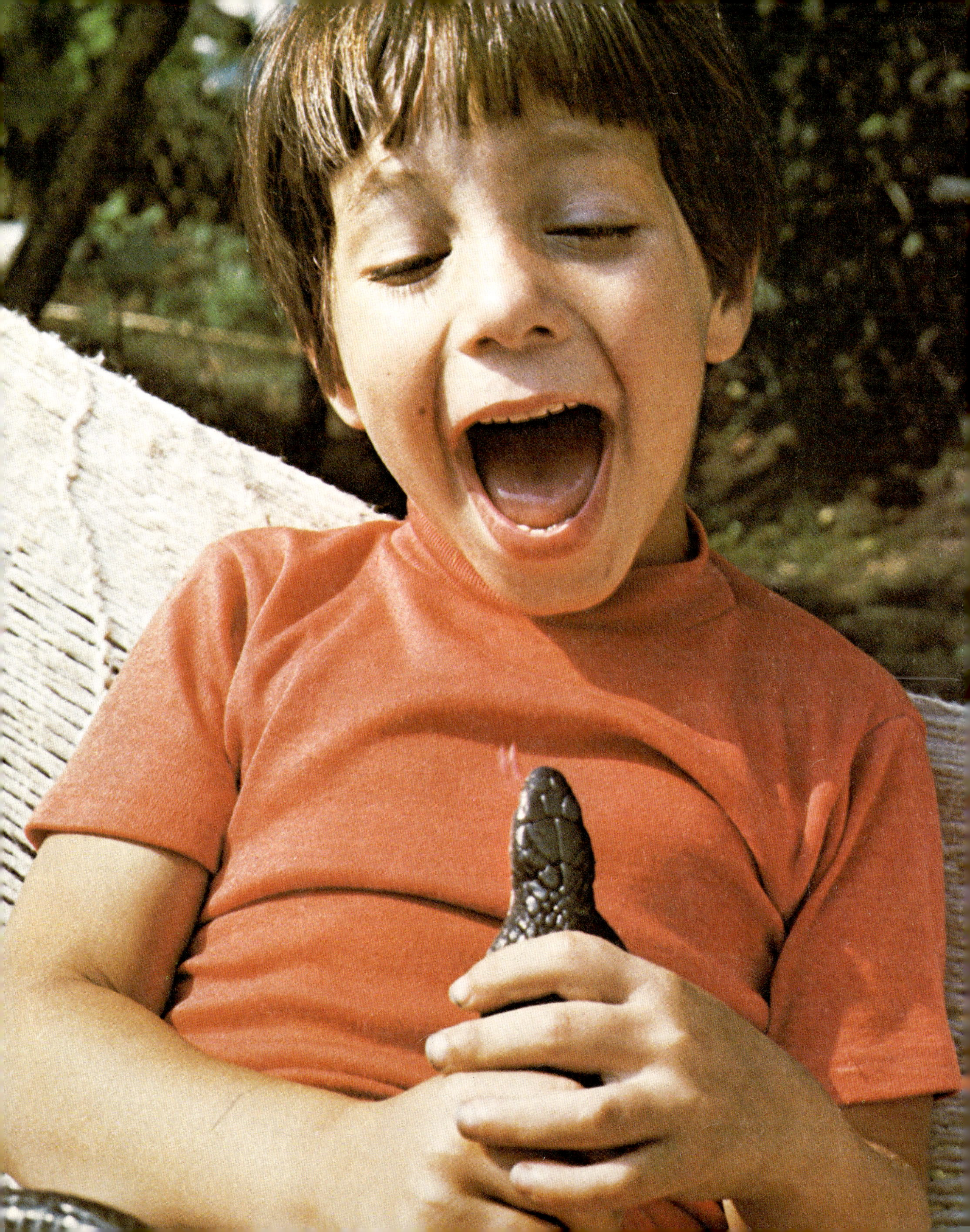

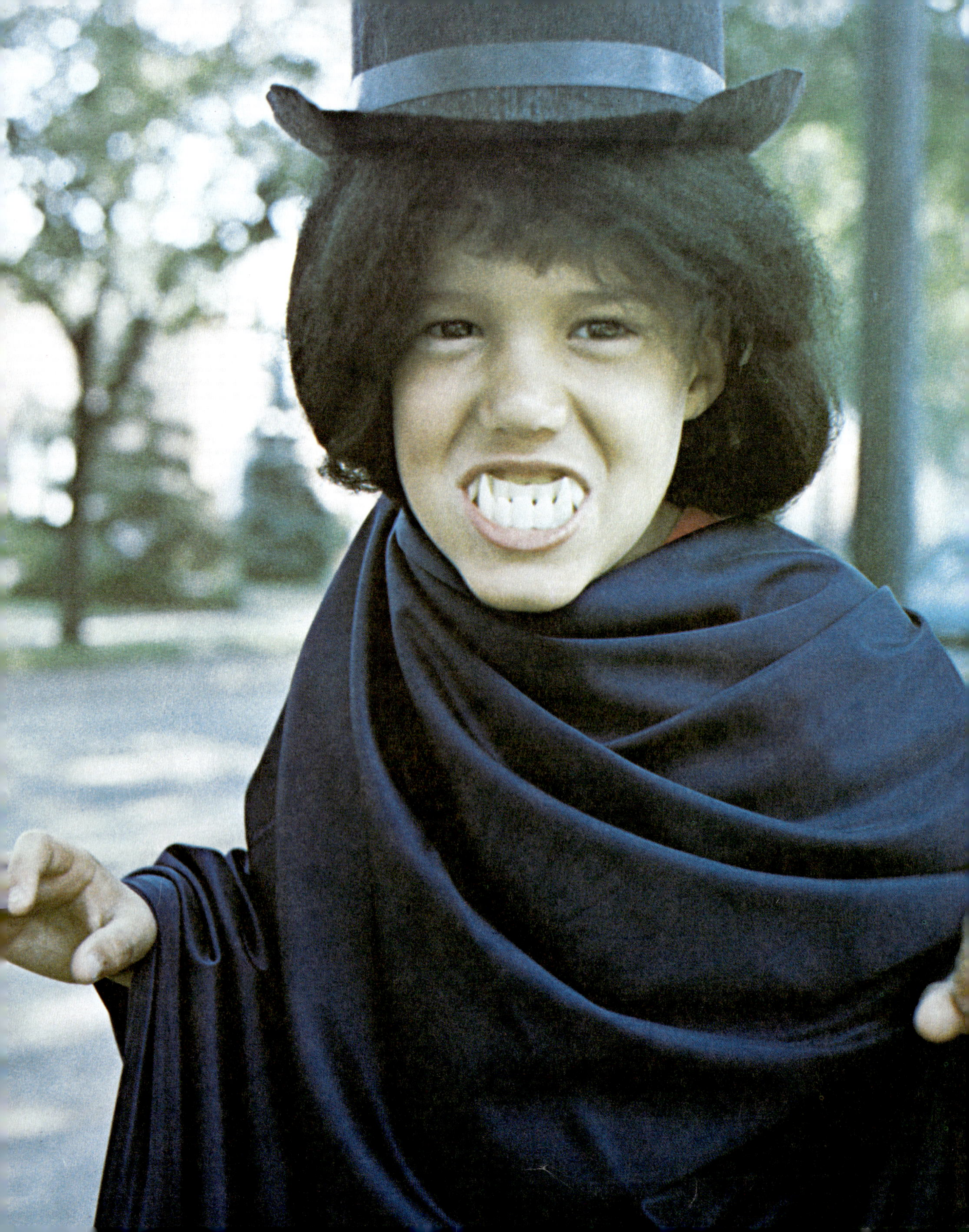

After that Tim kept trying to scare me. Tim knows that I am afraid of vampires. One time he got one of the big kids to dress up like a vampire.

In movies vampires come out at night and bite people on the neck. But I know vampires aren't real.

So I was not scared. Well, not very much. I knew it was just a joke.

Monsters don't scare me either. I know there's no such thing as a real monster. They are only in books and movies.

Oh, no, Tim! Look! Over your shoulder! Tim!

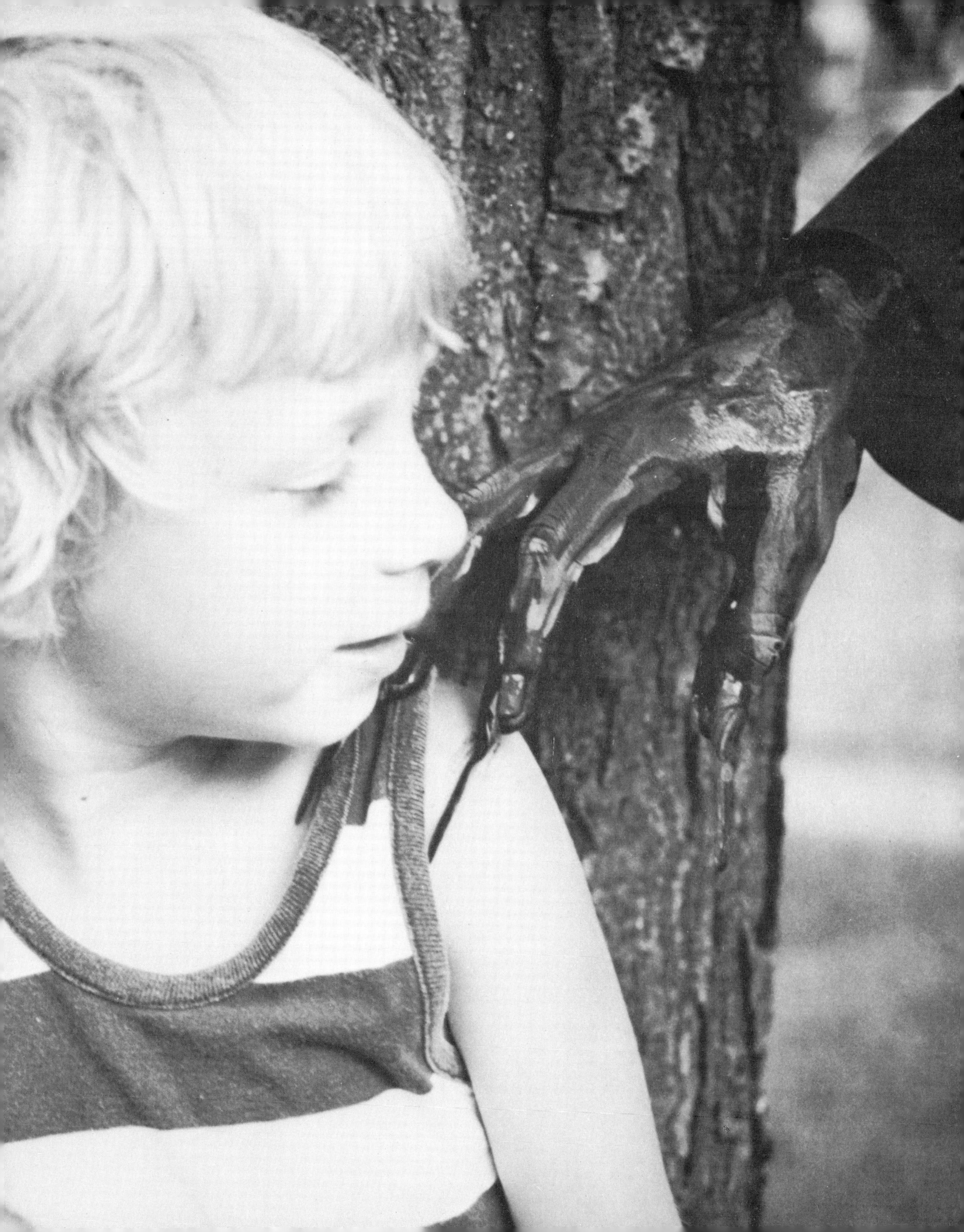